THE STORY OF NED KELLY

Copyright © 2023 by Aidan Phelan

All rights reserved. No part of this book may be reproduced in any manner whatsoever without written permission except in the case of brief quotations embodied in critical articles and reviews or for educational purposes.

First Printing, 2023

ISBN: 978-0-6457001-2-1
ISBN (eBook): 978-0-6457001-3-8

Australian history
Biography
Juvenile non-fiction

For more information on Australia's notorious bushrangers check out aguidetoaustralianbushranging.com

Special thanks to Erin Hutchinson, Neal Carney, Olivia Sweeney and family, and, of course, my wife Georgina for their assistance in bringing this book to fruition.

The Story of Ned Kelly

AIDAN PHELAN

Australian Bushranging

CONTENTS

1	Ned's Early Years	1
2	The Bushranger's Apprentice	5
3	Breaking the Law	11
4	Going Straight	17
5	Horse and Cattle Stealing	23
6	The Fitzpatrick Affair	27
7	Stringybark Creek	31
8	The Euroa Bank Robbery	36
9	Sympathisers Targeted	42
10	The Jerilderie Raid	46

11	The Gang Disappears	51
12	The Death of Aaron Sherritt	58
13	The Glenrowan Siege	62
14	Ned Kelly on Trial	71
15	The End of Ned Kelly	74

Glossary 79
Bibliography 83
Places to Visit 87

| 1 |

Ned's Early Years

Edward Kelly, better known by his nickname, "Ned", was born sometime between 1854 to 1856, but there are no records that have been found to prove exactly when he was born. The place where he was born is also unknown. Some say he was born at his grandparents' farm in Wallan, or at the family home in Beveridge. What is known for sure is that he was the third child of John "Red" Kelly, an Irish convict, and Ellen Quinn, who had come to Australia with her family from Ireland as a free settler.

John had been sent to Tasmania as a convict for stealing pigs. It was not his first crime, but it was a particularly bad one because of the difficulties of living in Ireland in those days for the farmers who relied on their stock and crops to survive. When John finally gained his freedom, he decided to settle in what would later be called Victoria, which is how he met Ellen Quinn and her family.

Their first baby, Mary Jane, died when she was only a few months old, which was common in that time because it was hard to get medicine and there was rarely a doctor close by. The second child was a daughter they named Anne. After Annie and Ned, came Margaret (Maggie), James (Jim), Daniel (Dan), Catherine (Kate) and the last would be Grace.

They all lived on a small block in the town of Beveridge where John built a small house, which is still standing. John would do a lot of different jobs to make enough money to look after the family, such as splitting logs to sell for firewood or fencing, which were skills he taught to Ned. Times were tough and there was not enough money to keep the family fed, clothed and housed properly.

Ned and his siblings attended school at the church near home. Here Ned learned the basics of how to read and write, as well as maths and geography. He was known to be sporty and enjoyed playing with the other children.

In 1864, the family left Beveridge and moved to Avenel, closer to Ellen's family, where they tried to start a dairy farm. With so many mouths to feed and the farm not providing the money they needed, they became desperate and, of course, bad things followed.

In May 1865, John found a stray calf that belonged to one of his neighbours and, rather than return it to the owner, he killed it so that he could butcher it for meat. It was not a smart move. Although it was valuable food for his growing family it would mean big trouble if John was caught. The calf belonged to a farmer named Morgan who told the police that he suspected that the former convict, Kelly, had stolen the animal, and the police soon came looking for the calf. They discovered the hide and John was arrested. He was put on trial, and he was found guilty of the illegal possession of a cow hide and sent to Kilmore Gaol for six months. However, he only spent four months in gaol and got out just in time for his daughter Grace's birth.

While Ned's dad was in gaol, he did something very courageous. Ned spotted a local boy named Dick Shelton struggling in Hughes Creek and at risk of drowning. Ned went into the water and dragged Dick to safety. As the story goes, Dick's father was so grateful he gifted Ned a green silk sash with gold fringes on the ends. He would carry the sash with him for the rest of his life and the Sheltons would always pass down the story of how Ned had saved young Dick from drowning.

Ned's green sash with gold fringes.

When John was freed from prison, he soon became unwell. He began to drink a lot of alcohol, which made him very sick, and on the day after Boxing Day in 1866 he died. Because Ned was twelve years old, and he was the eldest son, he had to go all the way into town to notify the authorities. John was buried in the cemetery at Avenel.

Ellen Kelly decided she needed to be even closer to her family so they could help her out now that she was a widow with seven children to look after. She moved into an old pub in Greta with her sisters and their children. All three women were without their husbands, but Ellen was the only widow. Her sisters had married two Lloyd brothers who were both in prison. The Kelly children must have enjoyed living with their Lloyd cousins, but the fun was cut short when one night the pub burnt down because it had been set on fire by Uncle James Kelly as revenge for a fight he had with Ellen.

After trying very hard to get approval, Ellen was allowed to lease a selection in Greta. This meant that she did not own the land her family was living on and had to pay rent, as well as keep the selection cleared and fenced and farmed. It would be hard work, but she now had her own place to raise her family. It was tough for a widow and her children, but they had no choice if they wanted to survive, and everyone had to pitch in.

However, Ellen soon found it difficult to keep on top of her rent payments. She made some money by letting travellers stay in the house and selling "sly grog", which meant selling alcohol without a licence. Ned tried to help out but it was time for him to get a job so he could contribute to the household more.

Ellen Kelly.

| 2 |

The Bushranger's Apprentice

Ned worked odd jobs like his father, but the family needed more money than he could earn that way. One of the ways Ned would make money was to look for lost horses and cattle. Sometimes he would find an animal and hide it until a reward was offered for its return, then he would take it in to the police or the pound. Sometimes the animals were not exactly missing before Ned found them, but he kept that bit secret.

Ned's uncles were friends with a local bushranger named Harry Power who was looking for an assistant due to his age and health problems. The now 15-year-old Ned began working for Power around 1869, looking after the horses and doing chores around the camp. In return Ned would get a share of the takings from Power's robberies and learn valuable bush skills.

Sometimes Ned was even allowed to help Power with his robberies, although he was usually holding horses in the bush out of sight. Harry was a gruff, aggressive bandit who would happily rob men, women, and children. He refused to use violence although he often threatened to. They never made much money as they usually robbed random travellers, rather than mail coaches or gold escorts like the bushrangers Ned admired such as Ben Hall and Dan Morgan.

Harry Power

During his time with Harry Power, Ned picked up some bad habits such as smoking a pipe, which was considered a dirty habit by many people even in those days. And because Harry's hideout was up in the mountains of the King River Valley, there was not much of a chance to have a good scrub, so Ned began to look very dirty. He quickly learned that Harry Power was a very grumpy old bushranger whose health problems made him very uncomfortable, and he would take out his unhappiness on Ned. Power had bunions on his feet that were so bad he had to wear boots that were so big they curled up at the toes just so he could walk around without being too uncomfortable. He also had a bowel stricture which meant he had a lot of trouble going to the toilet.

One day while eyeing off some good horses at Mount Battery station, Power and Kelly were spotted by the owner who shot at them with his shotgun. The blast almost hit Ned and he froze with fear, but he regained his composure quickly and escaped with Harry. Shortly after this Ned decided to leave Harry Power and go home. He realised the little bit of money he got from helping the old bushranger wasn't worth the abuse, the danger and being constantly hungry and filthy. He went back to his mother and decided to try making money some other way.

On October 14, 1869, Ned's sister Annie noticed a Chinese man by the gate carrying a large stick and a billy can. The man's name was Ah Fook and he was a farmer from Morse's Creek who was tired and thirsty from being on the road. He asked for water, although he could not speak English. Annie fetched him water from the creek, and he began to abuse the girl and waved his fist in her face threateningly. Ned, who was assisting some men his mother had brought in to help on the farm named William Gray and William Skillion, saw the argument and intervened. He began to yell at Ah Fook, allegedly saying that he was a bushranger and would rob him, and then chased him around. During this, Ah Fook's purse was dropped to the ground. There was a scuffle and Ned struck Ah Fook with the large stick that he had been carrying over his shoulder, leaving welts and bruises on his body. Ah Fook ran away, and Ned thought was the last he would hear of him.

Soon Ah Fook made a report to the police that Ned Kelly had beaten and robbed him and showed them the injuries. The police went to Mrs. Kelly's selection to arrest Ned, and when Annie spotted them coming, she went inside and warned Ned who immediately tried to run away to escape. He was very quickly cornered by the troopers, Sergeant Whelan and Constable McInerney, and nabbed for assault and robbery.

Ned complained that if the fence was just a little closer, he could have gotten away.

The case went to trial and Ah Fook needed an interpreter so that his evidence could be translated into English. Unfortunately for Ah Fook, Ned had more witnesses to back him up and, in the end, because there was not enough evidence to prove the charges he was let off, even though people believed he was probably guilty. The police were now aware that Ned had the potential to be a troublemaker like his uncles and they would be waiting for him to slip up so they could teach him a lesson.

At the beginning of 1870 Ned teamed up with Harry Power again. They did a small number of robberies together, including robbing a magistrate named Robert McBean on his own property in and taking his prized pocket watch. Although Ned was there, McBean could not get a good look at him.

A story would later be passed around that Harry Power had ordered Ned to steal some of the cattle from the Moyhu pound. In the middle of the night the pound keeper caught Ned on horseback trying to open the gate. He pulled Ned out of his saddle and threw him on the ground, then he began to whip him over and over with a riding crop. Ned escaped, but a few weeks later he and Harry bailed up the pound keeper and threatened to shoot him as revenge, but he was let go.

After leaving Power for good, Ned headed home and probably went straight to bed to catch up on some much-needed rest after all the bushranging. On the morning of May 4, he was woken by police who had come to arrest him on suspicion of being Power's accomplice.

Ned went to trial on two charges of aiding a robbery, and again he was not convicted because there was not enough evidence to prove it was him. The newspapers reported that even though he was not found guilty it was well known that he had been helping Power and it made him something of a celebrity among the young men around Beechworth and Greta. Ned loved the attention but not for long.

He was sent to Kyneton over another charge related to his time with Power. He was interrogated by Superintendent Nicolson and Superintendent Hare about what he knew about Harry Power, but none of the information he gave was ever useful. After Ned was discharged from court due to yet another case not being proven against him, it was reported that he was still seen in Kyneton days after because he was waiting for someone to pick him up or send him money to cover his expenses to get home by himself. He occupied himself with helping out at the police station.

While Ned was on trial in Kyneton, Harry Power was finally caught. Ned's uncle Jack Lloyd had made a secret deal with the police to show them to Power's hideout. Jack led them part of the way then met with Power in secret and returned to the police with Robert McBean's watch as proof that it was the real hideout. Lloyd then left the police to find their own way up the mountain to the camp because he was worried what would happen if people found out he had helped them. The Aboriginal police tracker pointed to smoke from Power's campfire and after much travelling on foot in heavy rain without food and very little rest, the police finally reached the camp. They found Power asleep in his hut and dragged him out by his feet and arrested him. The police then sat around the fire and ate Power's food rations while he complained about being caught.

When news got out that Power had been caught, many believed Ned had dobbed him in. In fact, the newspapers published a rumour that he had disguised himself as an Aboriginal man to act as a tracker for the police without being recognised, but this was easily proven false. Ned soon found himself in a very uncomfortable position because he was seen as an untrustworthy "dobber" or "snitch" by many people, and a no-good hooligan by others.

He wrote to Superintendent Nicolson and Sergeant Babington at the Kyneton police station and asked for help because the way others saw him made it hard for him to get by and raise money for his family. He said that everyone looked at him "like a black snake". Ned did not receive any reward money from Power's capture, but his uncles did.

Ned Kelly, aged 15.

| 3 |

Breaking the Law

Ned did not stay out of trouble for long. It was only a few months before his short temper and refusal to control his behaviour saw him back in court. This time it was over a rivalry he had gotten in the middle of.

On October 30, 1870, a hawker named Ben Gould had gotten his wagon bogged because of heavy rain and went to Ned's uncle Jack Lloyd for help. He recognised the horse that they used to pull the wagon out belonged to his rivals, the McCormacks. Ned, who happened to be there at the time, took the horse back to the McCormacks who accused him of stealing the horse and gear, which he denied. During the argument Ned mentioned his uncle Jack, who the McCormacks began to accuse of having stolen their property.

When Ned went back, he told everyone what had happened, and Gould decided to send the hawkers a nasty letter with a parcel full of parts from the cattle they were butchering. He gave the parcel to Ned to deliver to the McCormacks, and Ned told one of his Lloyd cousins to do it for him. This young Lloyd told the McCormacks that the parcel was from Ned Kelly and when they discovered what was in it, they were, naturally, very upset. Jeremiah McCormack confronted Ned and there was an argument during which Ned tried to scare Mr. McCormack away by riding his horse very close to him. In the heat of the moment Mrs. McCormack threw a stick at Ned and hit his horse instead. Ned struck McCormack in the face, knocking him down and later said it was caused by Mrs. McCormack hitting his horse, which caused it to rear up and his fist accidentally collided with Mr. McCormack's nose.

Ned was put on trial in Wangaratta and found guilty of assault and indecent behaviour. For hitting Mr. McCormack, he was sent to Beechworth Gaol for three months, and because he couldn't afford to pay the fine for sending the offensive parcel to Mrs. McCormack, he was given an extra three months, which meant that he had to spend the next half a year in Beechworth Gaol because of a silly fight he could have easily avoided.

It would have been a scary time for Ned, who would have grown up hearing stories of the horrors that the convicts had to suffer in prison and may have even heard his father talk about his own experiences. In those times every person convicted of a crime went to the same gaol, no matter if they were children or adults, and it made no difference how severe the crime was. For this reason, many people thought prisons were just a way for young criminals to be taught by the older ones how to cause more trouble. It is not hard to imagine how terrifying it would be for a teenage boy like Ned having to mix with hardened criminals in a prison that was already scary enough because of its reputation for harshness.

Luckily for Ned, he only did four of his six months before being let out. As scary as it may have been, it seems that gaol did not change Ned's behaviour, because when he got out of Beechworth Gaol it was barely weeks before he was in trouble again. A man named "Wild" Wright, a family friend, had supposedly lost his horse. He told Ned about it when he had stopped by the Kelly selection for some of Ellen's sly grog, and arranged to borrow one of Ned's horses, promising to return it when the other horse was found. Ned later located the horse and rode it into town. He was quite proud of how nice the horse was and showed off, taking some of the girls he fancied for a ride.

What Ned didn't know was that Wild had a habit of borrowing other people's horses without permission and this particular horse had been taken from the postmaster in Mansfield. Unfortunately, this meant that when he rode the horse past the police station, Senior-Constable Hall immediately thought it was stolen because it matched the description of one he had read about in the *Police Gazette*, which was a special newspaper that kept the police up to date on crimes that had been committed. He went outside and tried to get Ned to come down from the horse so he could arrest him, saying he had papers from Beechworth Gaol in the station for Ned to sign. When Ned refused to get down, Hall dragged him off the horse. Ned refused to go quietly, and they wrestled. In the chaos, Hall pulled his revolver out and tried to shoot Ned, but it jammed. Eventually, Hall got some men to hold Ned down while he beat him over the head with his revolver. Ned was very badly hurt, and a doctor came to the lock-up and sewed up his head wounds. The doctor told Hall off for being so rough and Hall would later get in trouble from his superiors for injuring his prisoner.

Ned went back to court on a charge of horse stealing, but it was soon proven that the horse had been taken while Ned was still in gaol. Ned was instead charged with receiving a stolen horse and found guilty. He was sentenced to three years in gaol.

Ned wrestles with Senior-Constable Hall

For the first few months Ned was back in Beechworth Gaol, but then he was sent to Pentridge Prison in what is now called Coburg. Pentridge was where Ned's old bushranging mentor Harry Power was doing time and was a huge prison with bluestone cell blocks and walls that almost looked like an old mediaeval fortress. It was a very unpleasant place to be.

At the beginning of his stay at Pentridge, Ned was kept apart from other prisoners and had to be silent. When he was out of his cell, he had to wear a hood that covered his face so nobody could recognise him and could only talk with the guards using sign language. He also had to go to church on Sundays and go to a school in the prison during the week to learn reading, writing and maths.

At Pentridge, the main work for the convicts was breaking bluestone, which was used for building and paving the roads, but there were also workshops where they could weave cloth, make items from wood and even a tailor shop where clothing could be made and mended. This was to make sure the inmates had useful skills when they finished serving their sentence so that they could find a good job and stay out of trouble. Punishments for bad behaviour could be very harsh and were things like getting smaller food rations or solitary confinement. If prisoners were really badly behaved, they might be placed in a box and put in a hole in the ground for a few days, with only a tiny slot where they could be given bread and water, or they might even be flogged with a cat-o-nine-tails. Luckily for Ned, he was smart enough to behave himself.

Ned proved he was a hard worker, and he was sent to Williamstown where he was kept on the prison hulk *Sacramento*. Many of the well-behaved Pentridge inmates were sent to Williamstown because they were good workers, and their behaviour was easier to control. Every day Ned would be rowed to the beach at Point Gellibrand and had to work on the seawalls. Later he was sent to the military barracks at Fort Gellibrand, which was close by, to help repair the military buildings. In all the time he was there he never missed a day of work, except for a few days right at the end when he had a tummy ache and got permission to rest from the doctor.

As a reward for his hard work and good behaviour Ned was released from prison three months early in February 1874. He had now grown into a strong, tall young man with more skills and knowledge than before, which would be useful for him when looking for work. He headed back to Greta and his family who he had not seen or heard from in almost three full years.

Ned Kelly in his prison uniform

| 4 |

Going Straight

When he got back home to Greta a lot of things had changed. His brother Jim was in gaol in New South Wales for helping to move stolen cattle. His big sister Annie had died after having a baby and the baby had died soon after. His sister Maggie had married William Skillion, the man who had been working on the Kelly selection for Ellen and was pregnant. He found all of his horses were missing and was told that a local police constable named Ernest Flood had stolen them and sold them to the men working on the north-eastern railway. On top of all of this, his mum had a new boyfriend named George King and, almost as soon as Ned was home, they got married. The family then welcomed in three new half-siblings: Ellen, John and Alice. It was a lot for Ned to take in.

George King was very mysterious. He was said to have been from California, but nobody is sure who he really was. It is possible he lied about being American to hide his identity as there are no records that show someone with that name arriving in Australia from California. When he married Ellen Kelly, he said his age was twenty-five years old, which made him only a few years older than Ned. He may have been a prospector who was in search of a place to mine for gold, but the gold rush in the region had ended long before 1874.

Ned Kelly boxing in front of a crowd.

Ned picked up a number of different jobs once he was a free man. One of these was said to have been as a stonemason in Chesney Vale as part of a crew that was building houses, which included his little brother Dan. Ned also said that he worked at a sawmill for Saunders and Rule, then as an overseer for Heach and Dockendorf. By Ned's own account he earned £2/10s a week, which was very good money for the time.

In August of 1874, nineteen-year-old Ned settled the score with Wild Wright. They fought each other in a boxing match that went for twenty rounds and Ned won. To commemorate the event, Ned posed for a photograph dressed in his underwear with silk boxer shorts over the top, and slippers. The details of the match were written on the bottom of the photograph. Later Wild Wright would tell people that Ned Kelly gave him the thrashing of his life.

Ned's feelings about the police had not improved in all the time he was in gaol. In fact, his experiences since that fight with Senior-Constable Hall were making it worse. But, despite his hatred for the police, in about 1877 he befriended a young local constable named Alexander Fitzpatrick. Fitzpatrick was seen as a larrikin and often mixed with people he probably shouldn't have. He would have been given a stern talking to by his boss if they knew he was friendly with the notorious Kellys. It was said that he had a crush on Kate Kelly who was only a young teenager at the time.

Since Maggie had moved into a new home nearby with her husband Bill Skillion and begun to raise her own family, Kate was now the eldest daughter in the house and had many more responsibilities to help her mum. The boys, Ned and Dan, were often away for long periods of time for work.

Ned Kelly in work clothes.

Dan was known to pick up various seasonal jobs, such as shearing sheep. He often spent his free time riding his horse and hunting for kangaroos. He got into trouble over a saddle he was accused of stealing, and when he showed the receipt for it in court as proof that he had bought it fair and square the case was dismissed. Ned had been in court as a witness to vouch for his brother.

Not long after, Dan was in trouble again, but this time it was with his cousins Tom and Jack Lloyd because they had all gotten drunk and broken into a shop where they caused chaos. Constable Fitzpatrick asked Ned to convince Dan and the Lloyds to turn themselves in, which he did. Dan and Jack Lloyd went to Beechworth Gaol for three months each, while Tom Lloyd was sentenced to six months because he had assaulted the woman who ran the shop, although he got out early.

It seemed like wherever the family were, police trouble was not far away because the police had instructions to immediately arrest them over any offence, no matter how small the crime or how trustworthy the information they had was.

It was during this quiet time in Ned's life that his family's problems with the local squatters began to get worse. There were often stories about poorer farmers getting their animals impounded by the squatters and not being able to afford the pound fees, which were close to a week's wages or more in many cases. Often the squatters were angry that they had been made to give up a portion of the land they had taken so that poor farmers could lease it from the government, and they would do things that they thought would force these undesirable people to leave the area. It was believed by the Kellys and their associates that the police were being secretly bribed by squatters to pick on the selectors they didn't like.

One of the squatters the Kellys knew well was a man named James Whitty. He was an Irishman who had settled at Moyhu, near Greta, and started a sheep farm. His wife had been known to sometimes baby-sit for Ellen Kelly in the past, but, at some point, there was a falling out and Whitty and his son-in-law James Farrell became Ned's enemies. Ned said it was because they accused him of stealing cattle from them, which he did not do. He also said he confronted Whitty at the races about a rumour he had spread that Ned had stolen a bull from him, but the problem continued. Ned decided that if the squatters wanted something to complain about, he would give it to them.

| 5 |

Horse and Cattle Stealing

In 1877 Ned began to break the law again. Horse stealing was a big problem in the northeast of Victoria, especially around the Murray River and the border of New South Wales, and Ned decided this was the way to get back at those people who he thought were greedy or bullies. Whether they were squatters or selectors was not important if he felt like they had done the wrong thing. He would steal their prized horses and sell them for a profit, often in towns over the border where it was harder for police to track him.

It is not known exactly who was involved in helping him because it was kept secret to stop the police arresting them, but according to Ned he was assisted by his stepfather, George King, who he said was an even better horse thief than him. It was later revealed that Ned was also helped by Joe Byrne and Aaron Sherritt, who he had recently met. It was also believed they were assisted by members of the Greta Mob to move the horses as many of them knew ways to get around the country without being spotted or recognised.

The Greta Mob was a gang of young larrikins from Greta and its surrounding towns, and it included many friends and relatives of the Kellys. They were considered a nuisance in the district because of their often rowdy and criminal behaviour. They swore a lot, loved fast horses, smoked pipes, drank alcohol and dressed like "flash squatters" with high-heeled boots, red sashes around their waists, and their hat chinstraps under their noses.

Steve Hart dressed in the style of the Greta Mob.

When the horse thieves went into a town, they used fake names and pretended to be horse dealers shifting their stock so they could make a sale. They pretended to sell the horses to each other so that the locals could witness what they would think was a proper, legal sale. They could then use the fake receipt to "prove" they owned the horses legally when they really sold them. They would also alter the brands to make it harder to identify the horses. Aaron Sherritt was taught many duffing tricks by a crooked pound keeper he worked for, including how to make a fake brand look old by pricking the horse's skin with a needle dipped in iodine. This was all very successful, and they made a lot of money selling stolen animals without ever being caught, and drove the squatters mad in the process.

However, the police soon discovered some of the stolen horses were being sold by two German brothers named Baumgarten. They had bought the horses from a man who called himself Thompson, who may have actually been Ned Kelly, and had resold the animals without realising they were stolen. The Baumgartens were sent to prison while those who had stolen the horses in the first place were never punished for the crime. Ned later said he felt sorry for the men who had been sent to gaol because of his crimes but did not actually do anything to try and help them or their families.

Once the thieves had made enough money, George King mysteriously disappeared and was not heard from ever again. Ned decided to stay quiet for a while so that his return home would not be noticed, and he could avoid any questions the police might have for him about the missing horses.

Around this time there was an incident in Benalla where Ned had had gotten drunk in a local pub and was arrested for riding his horse on the footpath. The next morning when he was being taken to court, he ran away from the police and tried to escape arrest. Four policemen chased him into a bootmaker's shop and there was a fight. During the brawl a constable named Thomas Lonigan badly hurt Ned and this made him so angry that he was said to have told the constable, "I've never shot a man, but if I ever do, you'll be the first!" Ned eventually allowed himself to be handcuffed and taken across the street to the courthouse where he was fined for his terrible behaviour. One of the policemen involved in the fight was Constable Fitzpatrick, who Ned now saw as an enemy.

Constable Alexander Fitzpatrick

| 6 |

The Fitzpatrick Affair

On April 15, 1878, Constable Fitzpatrick was supposed to go to the Greta police station to take charge. Instead of going straight there he decided to try and arrest Dan Kelly who he had heard was suspected of horse stealing. Dan had not actually stolen the horses, but Constable Fitzpatrick did not know that.

When he arrived at Mrs. Kelly's house, Dan was not home so he decided to wait for Dan to return instead of going to the police station like he was supposed to do. After questioning the family's neighbour, Brickey Williamson, he returned to the Kelly house where he discovered that Dan had just returned from riding. When the constable told him that he was under arrest, Dan agreed to go quietly so long as he could finish his dinner first. What happened next is not known for sure as everyone who was involved told a different story.

Constable Fitzpatrick said that while he waited, there was an argument between himself and Mrs. Kelly, and at that moment Ned burst in with Brickey Williamson and William Skillion and all of them had revolvers aimed at him. He then said that Mrs. Kelly hit him on the head with a shovel and Ned shot him in the wrist; Dan Kelly restrained him, and he was later made to cut the bullet out of his arm and was forced to promise not to tell anyone what had happened.

Mrs. Kelly attacks Fitzpatrick with a shovel.

Ned Kelly had a very different version of the story because he claimed he was never even there in the first place. Some people said the fight started because Fitzpatrick was drunk and had tried to kiss Kate Kelly.

Because of Fitzpatrick's story, Ellen Kelly was arrested with her baby, Alice, and Williamson and Skillion were arrested too. They were all charged with aiding attempted murder, as Fitzpatrick's story made it seem like they were all trying to kill him. Ned and Dan had already gone into the bush to hide from the police at Dan's hut in the Wombat Ranges. Ned would later say that they mined for gold and distilled whiskey to try and raise money for a good lawyer to defend their mother in court.

After many months of waiting, when Mrs. Kelly and the two men were put on trial, they were found guilty. Mrs. Kelly was sent to gaol for three years, and Williamson and Skillion were sent to gaol for six years each. A lot of people were very upset by the news, especially because Mrs. Kelly had baby Alice to look after. Luckily, Maggie was able to take the baby to look after before their mother was sent to Melbourne Gaol. Kate now had to look after her younger siblings, although Maggie would often come over to help as she lived close by.

Now that the others had been found guilty, the police looked even harder for Ned and Dan. Ned was wanted for attempted murder so there was a £100 reward for his capture. The police thought that because Ned was so dangerous, the reward would encourage people to help them catch him quickly. Dan was also wanted as Ned's accomplice and faced a harsh sentence if he was caught.

Dan Kelly.

The police would spy on the Kelly farm in case the brothers came back, and sometimes they would rush into the house and scare Kate and her siblings to try and get them to say where Ned and Dan were. They would leave the house in a terrible mess and destroy their food after searching everywhere for a sign that the brothers had been visiting or hiding weapons in the house. News about this would reach Ned and Dan through their friends and relatives about what was happening, which only made them angrier at the police.

| 7 |

Stringybark Creek

When Ned and Dan could not be found, the police in the area asked local people if they knew anything about where they could be. They soon discovered rumours that the brothers were hiding in the Wombat Ranges.

A team of police was sent from Mansfield to go into the bush to find and capture them. Ned Kelly was considered to be armed and dangerous, and the police were very nervous to be going into the bush to catch someone who they thought had already tried to kill a policeman and would probably do it again. The leader of the party was Sergeant Michael Kennedy, a brave Irish policeman who had a lot of experience looking for criminals in the bush. Also in the party were Constable Thomas McIntyre from Mansfield, Constable Michael Scanlan from Mooroopna who was Sergeant Kennedy's close friend, and Constable Lonigan from Violet Town who was the only one of the four who knew Ned Kelly.

Sergeant Michael Kennedy.

They set out early in the morning on October 25, 1878, and travelled all day until they decided to set up camp at Stringybark Creek. Little did they realize that they were actually very close to where the Kelly brothers were hiding out with their friends Joe Byrne and Steve Hart. Ned had found the tracks from the police horses earlier in the day and Dan had located their camp, but they decided to wait and see what would happen.

The next morning Sergeant Kennedy and Constable Scanlan set off to search for the brothers. Lonigan and McIntyre stayed at the camp. During the day McIntyre tried to shoot some parrots for dinner, but this accidentally warned the Kellys that the police were close and armed. Ned decided he would bail up the police camp to take their weapons and supplies away from them. He was scared that the police would find the hideout and shoot him, so he wanted to make sure he stopped them before they got a chance.

That afternoon Ned and his gang went to the police camp. They hid in the bushes and watched the police, waiting for the right moment to strike. When Ned was ready he signalled to the others and they all came out aiming guns at the police and shouted for them to, "Bail up!"

McIntyre surrendered because he could not defend himself, but Lonigan ran for cover so he would be able to put up a fair fight. Before Lonigan could fire his gun at the bushrangers, Ned shot him dead.

Constable Thomas Lonigan.

Ned began to ask McIntyre a lot of questions about what the other police were doing while the rest of the gang looked for things to steal from the camp. They even ate the fresh bread McIntyre had just made for his mates. McIntyre was terrified but he did everything he could to convince Ned not to attack Kennedy and Scanlan. Ned told McIntyre to get Kennedy and Scanlan to throw away their weapons and surrender when they returned, which happened soon after Ned had given the order.

Ned orders Constable McIntyre to force Kennedy and Scanlan to surrender.

When McIntyre told his mates to surrender because they were surrounded, Kennedy reached for his revolver. Ned stood up and fired. He shot Scanlan as his horse was trying to gallop away in fear from the commotion. The rest of the bushrangers emerged from their hiding spots and started firing too. Kennedy jumped down and started shooting at Ned. McIntyre got on Kennedy's horse as it tried to bolt and escaped. Sergeant Kennedy ran after McIntyre into the bush and Ned followed him. He badly injured the brave policeman before he shot him dead as well. Ned would later say that Kennedy was the bravest man he had ever met.

The bushrangers took money and valuables from the dead police and took all of their supplies before returning to the hideout. Ned took Sergeant Kennedy's gold pocket watch with him. This watch had been a special gift from people in the community to thank Kennedy for his excellent police work and it would be a long time before it was returned to his family.

Constable Michael Scanlan.

McIntyre was injured when he was knocked off Kennedy's horse by a low tree branch and decided to hide until it was safe to keep moving. That night, using the stars as a guide, he found his way through the bush, and the next morning he was able to raise an alarm. He was badly hurt and exhausted, but McIntyre joined the search party to guide them to the camp and help find his friends so they could be buried.

Even though Lonigan and Scanlan were found quickly, it was almost a week before Sergeant Kennedy could be found. The whole community was very upset at what had happened and tried to raise money for the widows and children of Lonigan and Kennedy because they knew how hard it would be for them to survive now. The police were buried in Mansfield Cemetery and a large monument was later built and placed in the town to remember them.

| 8 |

The Euroa Bank Robbery

Very quickly after the tragedy the government made a new law that let them declare Ned Kelly and his gang to be outlaws. This meant that they had a period of time to hand themselves in to the police to face punishment for their crimes, and if they did not it would be seen as an admission of guilt, and anyone could shoot them dead for the reward that was offered. Because the gang refused to hand themselves in, they were declared outlaws and the reward for their capture, dead or alive, was £2,500. Anyone helping them risked going to gaol for fifteen years. If the outlaws were captured alive, they would all be hanged for murdering the police at Stringybark Creek, as that was the punishment for such a crime. Although Ned and Dan had been identified by Constable McIntyre, he did not know Steve Hart or Joe Byrne, so they were now outlaws even though their names were unknown.

Superintendent Nicolson was put in charge of the hunt for the bushrangers because he was one of the most experienced troopers in the police force. He stayed in Benalla and worked with Superintendent Sadleir, who was in charge of all of the police in the district.

Because they knew that police would come looking for them in the Wombat Ranges, the Kelly Gang tried to go into New South Wales. However, because of flooding they were unable to cross the Murray

River safely. They made their way to their friend Aaron Sherritt at Sheepstation Creek instead. They fired their guns into the air as a signal and Aaron took them to one of the old hideouts that he and Joe used to camp in.

A short while later, a large party of police led by Superintendent Nicolson, Superintendent Sadleir and Captain Standish went looking for the bushrangers at the Sherritt farm because their neighbours had told the police about the gang signalling to Aaron. When they couldn't find who they were looking for there they went to Mrs. Byrne's house because they knew Aaron was Joe Byrne's best friend. They asked Mrs. Byrne about the gang but she was no help. They also questioned Aaron Sherritt, who happened to be there at the time. He tried to strike a deal with Captain Standish, who was the highest-ranked policeman in Victoria, to save Joe's life. Standish agreed to protect Joe from being hanged if Aaron could convince him to turn Ned, Dan, and Steve in.

Ned remembered from his time with Harry Power that a bushranger needed lots of friends and supporters all over the country to help keep them safe from capture. This meant that sometimes they would have to pay people for their help, so Ned decided that they needed to get a lot of money to pay their supporters, and the best way to get a lot of money at once was to rob a bank. After weeks of research, they decided that robbing the bank in the township of Euroa was the best option.

They went to Younghusband's Station at Faithfulls Creek on December 9, 1878, where they bailed up everyone that was there. Ned went into the homestead to find the manager of the station and when the manager, Mr. McCauley, came in and asked him who he was, Ned said, "who do you think?" to which McCauley replied, "you could be Ned Kelly for all I know." Ned pulled out his revolver and informed the manager that he was a very good guesser before bailing him up too.

The gang's prisoners were locked up in a storeroom to stop them raising an alarm, except for some of the women who were allowed to stay in the homestead. One of the women at the station was Mrs. Fitzgerald, whose husband worked there, to whom Joe Byrne played the concertina while she did her chores.

A travelling salesman named Gloster arrived to camp at the station for the night and he and his assistant were bailed up too. The outlaws then helped themselves to new clothes and boots as well as perfume and cigars from the salesman's wagon. They wanted to make sure they were so well dressed that nobody would suspect them of being murderous bushrangers when they were travelling.

The next morning more people were bailed up, including a group of kangaroo hunters who mistook Ned for a policeman in plainclothes. After lunch, Ned, Steve, and Joe cut down the telegraph wires to stop any information about what they were up to reaching the police. Then Ned, Dan and Steve went into Euroa, leaving Joe to guard the prisoners by himself.

Because the bank would be closing for the day when they arrived Ned needed an excuse for the staff to let him in. Ned had made Mr. McCauley write out a cheque for him to take to the bank so that he could pretend he needed to cash it in order to get inside.

When they got to the bank Ned went to the front door while the others went around the back. Ned knocked on the door and told the staff inside that he needed to cash the cheque, but they told him the bank was closed and he should come again another day. Ned insisted that it had to be done that instant, and when the accountant opened the door to tell him to leave Ned pushed inside and pulled out his revolver. He made the staff empty out the cash drawer into a sack but when he tried to rob to the safe, he was told he needed to get the manager's key to open it.

Ned bails up the bankers.

Ned found the manager, Robert Scott, working in his office, where they were joined by Steve Hart who had come into the bank through the back. He had gone through the bank manager's residence where Scott's family was getting ready to go to a funeral. Hart had locked them all in one room with their servants before he went into the bank. One of the servant girls, Fanny Shaw, recognised Steve from when they were at school together. Dan was on guard at the back door to make sure nobody went in or out.

Mr. Scott told Ned he didn't have his key on him as it was in his study. Ned went into the house and demanded the key. Scott's wife,

Susy, searched the study and found the key for Ned who returned to the bank and cleaned out the safe.

Ned and Steve intimidate Robert Scott.

Ned made all the bank staff, the Scotts, and the servants come back to Younghusband's Station with them to make sure they didn't alert the police. The Scotts had so many children that Ned had to take an extra buggy to get everyone there. When Ned told Scott to go and prepare the buggy, Scott replied angrily that if he wanted it, he could go and harness it himself. Ned found this amusing and decided to do just that.

The gang kept their prisoners under close watch until late in the night. Ned told the prisoners about his life story and the crimes he had committed and blamed all of his troubles on Constable Fitzpatrick. Dan Kelly gave the watch he had stolen from Constable Scanlan to Gloster's assistant, and Joe put the finishing touches on a letter he had transcribed for Ned to be mailed to a politician they thought might help them before asking Mrs. Fitzgerald for some postage stamps.

When the time was right the gang left, splitting up to make it harder to follow them or work out where they were heading, and they made sure to show off how they could get their horses to jump over the tall fences as they rode at full gallop. Ned ordered everyone to wait two hours after the outlaws had left before leaving, and he threatened that if anyone disobeyed his orders he would come back and shoot them dead. The gang escaped with around £2000 in cash and gold.

| 9 |

Sympathisers Targeted

After the Euroa bank robbery, the government raised the reward for the capture of the Kelly Gang to £4000 and the police began to arrest people they thought might be helping the outlaws. Many of these people were kept in gaol for months and months while the police tried to find any evidence that they had been helping the gang, but they were unable to in most cases. Eventually they were ordered to release the people who had been locked up without having committed a crime. This made a lot of people in the community very angry at the police, especially those whose family members had been in prison waiting for their trial for months. Some people that had not been sympathetic to the Kellys were now starting to show support, and the people who were already on their side were even more supportive. From that point on, if people were upset with a policeman they would say, "I'll tell Ned about you!"

The Kelly sisters were also having a hard time with police. They were always being watched in case their brothers returned to the farm, and the police would burst into the house and destroy their food supplies while looking for hidden weapons, and threaten everyone in the house, including the children. It was said that the police would go into rooms while pushing one of the girls in front of them in case the outlaws decided to jump out and shoot at them, because if they did, they would accidentally shoot one of their siblings instead of the police. All of this added to the police being seen as bullies by those who supported the outlaws.

Maggie Skillion.

Ned began to think of himself as someone who could stand up for the people who had been mistreated by police. He believed the way he and his family had been treated was evidence that all police were bullies who were protecting the wealthy squatters and using their power to attack poor Irish families. He decided he should use the crimes he committed as a way to raise awareness of these issues as well as getting money for his supporters.

At the same time, people began to write songs about the gang that portrayed them as adventurous and daring. One of the people who wrote popular songs about the gang was none other than Joe Byrne, who was a talented poet and songwriter. These songs were sung all over the country and described the bushrangers as the opposite of how they were shown in the newspapers, where they were depicted in cartoons and news reports as ugly, nasty, and monstrous. Many poor people saw them as heroes for standing up to the rich and powerful who were making life hard for them, while the rich and powerful saw them as evil and inhuman because of their crimes. Many other people just saw them as dangerous criminals and hoped the police would capture them quickly so they could feel safe again.

It was very hard for the police to catch the gang because there were sightings reported in all kinds of places far apart from each other and it was sometimes hard to tell which ones were real. Most of the reports were either too old to be useful or were cases of mistaken identity. One report the police received said the gang were spotted travelling in a wagon and well-armed but when the police investigated, they found out it was just a cricket team on tour.

What made things even worse was that most of the police were not trained in bush work and were looking for the gang based on written descriptions of what they looked like. One time there were two police search parties in bush clothes that accidentally bumped into each other while searching for the outlaws and mistook the other for the Kelly Gang and they started shooting. Luckily nobody was killed or hurt during any of these events.

Moreover, everything the police were doing was being reported by the newspapers. All the outlaws and their supporters had to do was read the papers to find out what the police were up to, and they could avoid crossing their paths.

By the beginning of 1879 all the money the gang had stolen had run out too, so it was time for the Kelly Gang to strike again.

| 10 |

The Jerilderie Raid

It was in February 1879 that the Kelly Gang made their next move. This time they decided that not only would they rob a bank to get money for their families and supporters, but they would also embarrass the police in New South Wales at the same time. There was a rumour going around that the New South Wales police had bragged that the gang wouldn't last twenty-four hours if they crossed the border, and the Kellys decided to prove them wrong.

The gang crossed into New South Wales and headed to the township of Jerilderie. Ned and Joe got information about the town and its police from a barmaid at a pub just outside of Jerilderie called the Woolpack Inn, then the gang went to the police station. In the middle of the night on February 8, 1879, the gang woke the police up by bashing at the door and calling out that there had been trouble at the pub. When Senior-Constable George Devine and Constable Henry Richards answered the door, they were bailed up. The gang put the police in their own lock-up cell and used the police station as their headquarters while they plotted their next steps.

The following day Ned and Steve went into the town disguised as policemen and pretended to have been sent to protect Jerilderie from the Kellys. They took Constable Richards with them as a guide because Devine was harder to keep under control. This way they could see where everything was without attracting suspicion. Mrs. Devine was allowed to decorate the courthouse with flowers for the Sunday mass while one of the gang members guarded her.

When they were back at the police station, Ned and Joe put the finishing touches on a long letter that Ned wanted the local newspaper editor to publish. It was his side of the story about some of the crimes he had committed, including shooting the police at Stringybark Creek. He hoped this would encourage people to see things from his point of view and be a warning to anyone that might betray him or try to claim the reward money.

They used a map of the town to plot out their heist. Dan looked on, bouncing one of the Devine children on his knee. It was decided to use the hotel as a prison to stop the locals interfering in the robbery because it was next door to the bank. This may have given Joe an idea, and he rode back out to the Woolpack Inn and got terribly drunk.

Meanwhile, Ned read some of his letter to Mrs. Devine, but when she was asked what was in it by her husband she couldn't remember because she had not been paying attention.

The next day the outlaws put their plan into action. Dan and Joe dressed up as troopers and went into town. Joe got all of their horses shod at the blacksmith and the fee was charged to the government because the blacksmith thought he was putting shoes on the police horses.

Ned dictates his letter to Joe Byrne.

They were joined by Ned and Steve with Constable Richards, and they began to round up locals and held them prisoner in the pub with Dan guarding them. Then Joe went next door and stuck up the bank. He was soon joined by Ned and Steve.

The cash drawer was emptied but when they found the safe was locked Joe said they should smash it open with a sledgehammer instead of fussing around looking for a key like Ned had done at Euroa. Ned did not like Joe's idea and decided they should get the manager's key and sent Steve to fetch it.

Steve found the manager while he was having a bath and took his key and his watch. After they got all the money and valuables out of the safe, Ned stole records of some of the debts that people owed to the bank and burned them. He thought this would mean that the bank would not be able to make poor people pay them money anymore. Ned also told the local schoolteacher to give the students the day off school in honour of his visit.

THE STORY OF NED KELLY - 49

Ned disguised as a policeman.

After the bank was robbed, Ned gave a speech in the pub while Joe took some locals to help him sabotage the telegraph. Ned was upset to discover that while they were robbing the bank the newspaper editor had found out what was happening and ran out of town in fear. He had published some strong opinions about the outlaws in the local paper and he thought they would come after him for revenge. This meant Ned could not get his letter published. He gave the letter to a bank accountant named Edwin Living and told him to get it printed when the editor could be found.

Once again, the gang split up when leaving town. First, they rode up and down the main street shouting, "Hooray for the good old days of Dan Morgan and Ben Hall!" Then Dan and Joe headed off for Victoria while Ned and Steve stopped at one of the other pubs in town called the Traveller's Rest. While they were there, Ned put his revolver on the bar and challenged anyone to use it to shoot him if they had the guts.

Steve tried to steal Reverend Gribble's watch. When Gribble complained to Ned about the theft, Ned ordered Steve to return the watch. After an argument, Steve gave the watch back and they rode back to Victoria. As they were leaving, Ned threatened to come back and shoot anyone who raised an alarm.

Once again, they had stolen around £2000 worth of money and valuables, which was much less than the £10,000 Ned thought they would get. Many of the bank notes they stole were unmarked. In those days bank notes would have numbers written on them so they could be tracked, and because these did not have the numbers on them the police couldn't prove where the money came from. This made the robbery more of a success because it meant that there was no way to prove that the sympathisers had been getting money from the outlaws.

| 11 |

The Gang Disappears

Following the robbery in Jerilderie, the government of New South Wales were so angry and embarrassed about what had happened that they immediately doubled the reward that the Victorian government were offering. Having stopped the bushranging problem that had been rampant in the colony over many years during the gold rush, the authorities in New South Wales were very concerned that the Kellys could inspire another outbreak of bushranging. The doubled reward was now a total of £8000, which was enough money to keep a family living in comfort for many years.

In order to make the searches for the outlaws more effective, a team of Aboriginal trackers from Queensland, led by Sub-Inspector Stanhope O'Connor, were sent to join the pursuit. These were men from K'gari (also known as Fraser Island) who had advanced skills in tracking, and they soon became the only people that Ned Kelly was afraid of.

Parties of police would scour the bush looking for any trace of the outlaws. O'Connor felt that the senior police were slowing the search down and making it harder for him and his trackers to do their part. Sometimes when the police would have just started investigating a location where the trackers were finding clues, they would receive a telegram from Captain Standish ordering them to return to headquarters or follow a new lead.

To encourage the police to be more effective, their wages were doubled, and the government put as much money as they could afford, and all the extra police they could spare, into the hunt for the gang. Despite all the extra resources, and police in two colonies looking for them, the Kelly Gang seemed to be able to move around without fear of being spotted by any of them.

The newspapers also began to criticise the police for not being able to catch the bushrangers, and Ned Kelly claimed that it was because the police knew they would earn less money and have nothing to do once they had caught them.

Just before the gang went to Jerilderie, Superintendent Hare had taken over as the head of the hunt and was working with Aaron Sherritt, who had been giving information to the police. Based on Aaron's advice, the police had stationed a party to spy on Mrs. Byrne's house in the Woolshed Valley because he had said that the gang would go there to get supplies. What they did not know was that Aaron had deliberately told them to watch from a spot where they wouldn't be able to see the gang coming and going from the house. Aaron would often join the police as they watched the farm and told stories about his adventures with Joe Byrne and Ned Kelly. In these stories he would talk about how tough and clever Ned was and brag about the crimes they had committed. He hoped that this would make him seem reliable to the police so that they would keep paying him to give them information, and he could keep them distracted from catching his friends at the same time.

Superintendent Francis Augustus Hare.

Superintendent Hare's time leading the hunt was cut short because he badly injured his back when he tried to get his horse to jump over a gate and had landed badly. This meant that Captain Standish had to bring back Superintendent Nicolson to take charge again. Nicolson decided that he needed to do things differently. Instead of going out in the bush to search for the gang, he hired spies to give him information about the gang's movements. Some of these spies included Joe Byrne's old schoolmate James Wallace, Aaron Sherritt's brother Jack, and a schoolteacher from Greta named Daniel Kennedy. All of the spies were given codenames so that their identities would be kept secret. Despite all of the changes, the police were still no closer to catching the outlaws.

By now Ned and the gang had a lot of supporters all around the colony who helped them. They would provide them with food, clean clothes, fresh horses to ride, and newspapers. Sometimes the sympathisers would scout for them too, or even travel in groups of four on similar horses to the gang's in order to confuse the police, because it was well known that three of the gang rode bay horses and Joe rode a grey mare named Music.

Ned's sisters Maggie and Kate would often leave bundles of supplies for the gang in a hollow log at a secret location. Maggie was once spied on by police who were trying to catch her delivering supplies to her brothers, however Maggie was clever and knew she was being watched so led the police on a chase into the bush carrying a big bundle. When the police caught up to her she made a rude gesture at them and when they searched the bundle, they found out all she was carrying was laundry. The drop-off point remained a secret.

Life in the bush was very hard on the gang and they were often unwell. Ned picked up an eye infection on the way back from Jerilderie and suffered from back pain from spending so much time riding horses over long distances. They would usually hide in the Strathbogie Ranges and the Warby Ranges, although they sometimes camped at the Greta swamp. Nights in the mountains were very cold and harsh, and without beds they had to get comfy on the rocks. If they were lucky, they might find an old miner's hut to shelter in, but it was not much better than sleeping in the open. The terrain was rugged and difficult to access for people who were not familiar with it. They would often travel by foot as it was difficult to look after horses in the bush and even harder to hide their tracks.

The food they had to eat was not very good either. They would mostly have salted meat or preserves such as jam or pickled offal, as well as damper and tea. Fresh fruit and vegetables were hard for them to get, and they did not last very long. Sometimes they had condiments like mustard to put on their food and Ned would use the empty tins to carry bullets in.

Joe Byrne would often sneak into Beechworth at night to visit his girlfriend, who was a maid at the Vine Hotel, known as Maggie. This was a very dangerous thing to do so close to the police station, but because Aaron Sherritt had the police distracted at the Byrne selection most of the time it made it easier for the outlaws to move at night without being caught. It also helped that Joe's brother Paddy would dress up like Joe and ride a similar horse in another location so that it was harder for police to work out which one was the real Joe.

Joe Byrne.

By the middle of 1879 the gang had apparently vanished because sightings became rarer, and the police were still clueless. The money from the bank robberies was all gone and all the banks in Victoria were being guarded by armed soldiers to stop the gang robbing them.

Joe Byrne had devised a plan to avoid this problem by sticking up a bank manager at night and forcing him to let them into the bank and open the safe, but that wasn't Ned's style. He thought it was important for his reputation to commit robberies in broad daylight, right under the noses of the police, to show how bold and unstoppable he was.

Even though Ned wanted to make fun of the police, his fear of the trackers remained, and he was tired of being on the run. He began to believe that the gang would have to do something drastic to the police to make them call off the pursuit, and he would need to be bulletproof to do it.

The gang began to experiment with different materials to see what could stop bullets. What they found worked best was the thick steel mouldboards on a plough. They started to collect more of these curved iron plates either by stealing them or by having them donated by sympathisers. Then the next step was to figure out how to turn them into armour.

Nobody knows exactly how the armour was made as it was kept secret. There were rumours that blacksmiths who were friends of the outlaws helped them to build it, but the story handed down through the family was that Dan Kelly and Tom Lloyd made the armour in Greta. As the story goes, Tom and Dan used a bush forge to heat the metal and they would beat it into shape around a green log that was partially submerged in a creek to dull the sound of the hammer blows.

Each member of the gang had a suit of armour that consisted of a helmet, a breastplate, a backplate and an apron that covered their thighs. Ned's suit also had pieces that protected his upper arms. The armour weighed around 97 pounds, or 45 kilograms. Even after the metal had been heated and reshaped it was bulletproof against the weapons the police were using. This would allow the gang to commit robberies or other crimes without the fear of being shot dead.

There was one important weakness in the armour, though. In order to move around, the arms and lower legs were unprotected. Bullet wounds to their limbs would not kill them but would disable them. The outlaws did not believe they would need to worry about that.

Ned tries his armour on for the first time.

| 12 |

The Death of Aaron Sherritt

During the year 1879, Aaron Sherritt continued to give police information even though none of it was ever useful, and police began to suspect he was not being truthful to them. This wasn't helped when he suddenly seemed to be paying for things with unmarked bank notes like the ones stolen from the bank at Jerilderie. The watch parties at Mrs. Byrne's selection were stopped and Aaron was instead employed by Superintendent Nicolson as a spy. Although Aaron was not able to keep the police distracted with the watch parties anymore, he was determined to find other ways to keep his friends safe from capture. Aaron's interactions with the police were starting to be noticed by the sympathisers who then told the outlaws that he was an informant.

After many months without success, Captain Standish decided that he needed to take Superintendent Nicolson off the case. At the beginning of June in 1880 he was replaced once again with Superintendent Hare. When Hare returned, he found the police operation was a mess. He spent most of his time trying to sort out Nicolson's notes and immediately sacked most of the spies. When Daniel Kennedy told him that the gang were making bulletproof jackets using stolen farm equipment, Hare dismissed the report as nonsense.

Hare reinstated the party of police to watch the Byrne selection. However, this time there were police watching the Kelly selection in Greta and the Hart selection in Wangaratta as well. Aaron was once again brought in to work with the police watching the Byrnes from a cave above the selection, and he and his wife Belle moved into a hut near Sebastopol to be closer to the lookout spot. Every night Aaron went out with the police and walked to the police cave, and all day the police would stay in his hut sleeping.

Aaron Sherritt.

Because of the rumours that Aaron had betrayed them, Ned decided to use Aaron and the police who were living with him as part of his next big plan, which would be carried out on June 26, 1880.

On that night, Joe Byrne and Dan Kelly captured Anton Wick, a German man who lived near Aaron Sherritt and was well-known to Joe. They took him to Aaron's hut and Joe ordered him to knock on the back door and pretend to be lost. Dan went around the front to guard the other door in case anyone tried to escape.

Inside the hut, Aaron and the four policemen were getting ready to walk to the cave overlooking Mrs. Byrne's farm. When they heard the knocking, the police hid in the bedroom and Aaron answered the door. As Aaron was about to give Anton Wick directions Joe stood in the doorway and shot Aaron twice with a shotgun, killing him instantly.

For the next few hours Joe and Dan tried to get the police to come out of the bedroom and even sent Aaron's wife and her mother into the bedroom to convince them to leave, but instead the police pushed the women under the bed and continued to hide. Dan tried to start a fire to smoke the police out, but the logs were too wet. They even fired into the bedroom, but luckily nobody was hurt. Eventually they let Anton go home and they headed off for Glenrowan.

The intention was that news of the attack would reach the police in Benalla and they would immediately take a special train at full speed to Beechworth to pursue the gang. Because it was a Sunday, when no civilian trains were allowed to run, the only train going along the line would have to be a special train full of policemen. Between Benalla and Beechworth was Glenrowan, and here there was a bend in the track on a steep embankment where Ned and Steve would break the train line so that it would derail, go down the embankment and crash. The crash would take out most of the police who had been chasing the gang, and any of the survivors would be held hostage by Ned Kelly in exchange for the release of his mother, and any other sympathisers, from prison. Because there was no telegraph station in Glenrowan the gang would be able to commit their crimes without information getting out quickly, and they could make their getaway without anyone bothering them.

Ned's plan relied on the news of the murder at Sherritt's hut reaching Beechworth very quickly afterwards, but the police in the hut were so scared that the bushrangers were waiting in ambush outside that they refused to come out until daylight. The news did not reach Beechworth until after lunch the next day, which meant that it would take even longer for the police to get organised to investigate the murder.

| 13 |

The Glenrowan Siege

While Joe and Dan were at Aaron's hut, Ned and Steve were in Glenrowan trying to sabotage the train line, but they did not have the correct tools. They searched the town, rounding up anyone that they thought would be able to pull up the rails. After a few hours, and a lot of running around, the train line was broken by a gang of men who were held at gunpoint and the outlaws now had a large group of people they had to keep prisoner to prevent them escaping and raising the alarm. Among the prisoners was Ann Jones who owned and ran the Glenrowan Inn, and her teenage daughter Jane.

After Dan and Joe arrived, the prisoners were split up between the stationmaster's house, where Steve guarded the women and children, and the Glenrowan Inn, where the rest of the gang would guard the men. Steve was ordered by Ned to keep an eye on the stationmaster to make sure he didn't signal the train when it arrived to warn it about the danger. As the day went on and there was no sign of a train, the gang took more and more prisoners. Eventually, there were more than sixty people being held captive in the inn as well as the stationmaster's house.

One of the prisoners was the local schoolteacher, Thomas Curnow. When he discovered Ned's scheme he decided to try and stop it. He spent most of the day trying to convince Ned he was a supporter in the hope that he could persuade Ned to let him go. Many of his attempts to trick the outlaw were foiled, but he did not give up because he knew that if he did not do something to stop Ned then dozens of people would be killed.

To stop the prisoners getting bored and rowdy, a dance was held at the inn and sporting games were played. Mrs. Jones and her children served drinks and food all day and into the night. Jane Jones got very friendly with Dan Kelly, and he let her hold his pistol to help keep the prisoners under control. Mrs. Jones told Ned that she saved the best food for him.

In the meantime, it took many hours to arrange a special train to depart from Melbourne which would pick up Sub-Inspector O'Connor and his trackers, who were preparing to return home to Queensland when they found out they had been called back to Beechworth. On board the train were some reporters who would write about the hunt for the outlaws for the newspapers. Because it was taking so long, Superintendent Sadleir ordered a second train that would depart from Benalla in the evening with a party of police led by Superintendent Hare if the other one did not arrive in time.

That night, Ned decided to capture the local policeman, Constable Bracken. He took a small group to accompany Joe Byrne and himself, and after they had kidnapped Bracken, who had been sick in bed, Ned let Thomas Curnow take his family home. Before they left Ned warned Curnow that someone would be around later to make sure they were still at home. After taking his family home, Curnow wasted no time and got ready to stop the train by grabbing a candle and his sister's red scarf to use as a signal. Later, when he heard the train coming, he went to the train line, which was close to his house, and waited to flag down the engine when it arrived and warn the police of the sabotage.

Because the train from Melbourne had been damaged when it accidentally smashed through a gate that had been left open across the tracks, both engines were sent to Beechworth, but the damaged engine went ahead as a scout in case there were any other hazards on the track. The carriages from the damaged train were connected to the one that had been waiting at Benalla and it followed a safe distance behind the scout. When the first engine spotted Curnow's signal, it stopped and Curnow warned the driver about the damaged train line. The crew warned the following train and once the coast was clear both engines slowly and safely pulled up to the train station in Glenrowan.

In the early hours of Monday morning, Dan told the prisoners they could go home but Mrs. Jones stopped them leaving so that Ned could give a speech. He was interrupted by Joe and Dan telling him the train was coming. The gang went into a bedroom at the back of the inn to dress in their armour and Constable Bracken stole the key to the front door so he could escape. He ran to the train station where the train had just pulled up and told Superintendent Hare that the Kellys were in Mrs. Jones' pub. Hare then led his police across to where the Kelly Gang were waiting in front of the building in their homemade armour.

A gunfight immediately broke out. Superintendent Hare was wounded when he was shot in the wrist. He fired and reloaded his shotgun with only one hand but went back to the station to get the injury bandaged up. When he was heading back to the battle, Hare fainted from blood loss and had to be sent back to Benalla on the train to seek a doctor because his injury needed immediate care. The police surrounded the front of the inn and continued firing. Inside, the prisoners laid on the floor to try and avoid being shot by the police. Ann Jones' son John was badly wounded by a police bullet and a brave labourer, Jack McHugh, carried him to safety even though he was almost shot by police himself in his attempt.

The gang attack police from the front of the Glenrowan Inn.

Joe Byrne was badly injured when he was shot in the leg, and Ned was also shot in the foot and the left arm. When the gang ran out of ammunition they went around the back of the inn. Dan and Steve went inside to barricade the front of the inn while Ned and Joe discussed their situation outside. Ned decided to try and find an escape route so they could get away without the police following, but when he tried to mount Joe's grey mare the gunfire spooked her, and she galloped into the bush. Ned followed her on foot and passed out near a fallen tree because of his injuries.

Joe went into the inn with the others, and they continued to fight while trying to convince the police to stop shooting long enough for the prisoners to escape. The police did not listen and continued shooting. Young Jane Jones courageously led a group of women and children to safety while holding up a candle to light the way through the darkness. She had been wounded when a police bullet had hit her in the head, but she showed no sign of fear as bullets zipped past her.

About two hours into the battle, Joe went to the bar to have a drink and gave a toast to the outlaws, "Here's to many more days in the bush, boys!" At that moment a hail of bullets struck the inn and one of them managed to get through a tiny gap in Joe's armour and killed him. Now it was just Dan and Steve in the inn with the remaining prisoners.

Police reinforcements now began to show up, starting with a party from Wangaratta led by Sergeant Steele. Steele saw some of the prisoners trying to escape, and when they didn't stop at his command, he fired at them thinking they must be the outlaws trying to get away. Mrs. Reardon and her baby were nearly shot, and her teenage son was shot in the back by Steele as he retreated to the inn with his three-year-old brother. Another group of reinforcements arrived around the same time led by Superintendent Sadleir, who had taken over for Hare who was now back in Benalla getting his wrist treated by a doctor.

Just before dawn, Ned Kelly emerged from the bush behind the police. He began to fire his revolver and taunted them. Many of the police rushed over to see what was happening. Some of them were terrified because they could not tell through the mix of gun smoke, fog and the gloom what was attacking them and especially because it seemed to be completely bulletproof. Some thought it was a bunyip, others said it was the devil. As Ned continued to fight the police, bullets struck his unprotected limbs, wounding him. Whenever bullets hit his armour, it felt like being punched.

As he reached a large fallen tree, Sergeant Steele saw that Ned's knees were an unprotected weak spot and shot him there. Ned fell and was unable to get back up due to his injuries and the weight of his armour. The police swarmed on Ned. Steele tried to shoot him dead, but Constable Bracken stepped in to stop the him before it was too late. At that moment Dan and Steve tried to shoot the police that were around Ned, but they were too far away to be effective. Dan was shot in the knee, so they went back inside the inn.

Ned Kelly is finally brought down.

Ned's armour was removed, and he was carried to the train station where he was treated for his wounds. He had around thirty injuries from the bullets that were fired at him, and he had lost a lot of blood. The doctors did not think he would survive.

Soon Ned's family and supporters arrived, and the Kelly sisters were allowed to see him. The rails had been repaired and trains began to arrive carrying spectators who had heard that the outlaws were in Glenrowan fighting with the police. A portable telegraph was set up so that news could be sent to Melbourne to provide live updates. The police continued to fire into the inn and even more police joined them from Beechworth. Superintendent Sadleir arranged for a cannon to be brought up so that they could blast the inn open and capture any bushrangers still inside. He was afraid that if the police tried to go into the inn and capture them that some of them might be shot.

Ned Kelly after his capture.

By lunchtime the rest of the civilians had been allowed to come out of the inn, which left only Dan and Steve inside. In the kitchen was a civilian named Martin Cherry who had been shot in the stomach by a police bullet. At one o'clock in the afternoon Dan and Steve stopped firing back at the police and two hours later Superintendent Sadleir gave orders for the inn to be burned, as he hoped the smoke and flames would force the outlaws to come out.

Senior-Constable Johnston gathered the tools to set fire to the inn and almost got into trouble when he encountered some of the gang's supporters who had come to see what was happening. The sympathisers were carrying guns, and he thought that if they realised he was a policeman they would shoot him, so he pretended to just be an onlooker. As he approached the building, the police continued to fire into the inn in order to distract the outlaws. He set some straw on fire near the chimney, and it spread quickly.

A priest named Father Gibney rushed into the burning building to find any survivors who had been unable to escape. He found all three outlaws were dead. Joe was on the floor in the bar and the others in a bedroom. It was impossible to tell how Dan and Steve had died as it was too dangerous to investigate because of the fire. Joe's body was dragged out of the inn by some police who had gone in after the priest, but Dan and Steve were cremated in the fire. Their remains were given to their families for burial, but the police kept Joe's body, which they hung on a cell door in Benalla the next day so it could be photographed. In times past it was common for dead criminals to be put on display for people to look at as a warning to anyone else who was thinking of taking up a life of crime.

As well as the outlaws, John Jones and Martin Cherry died from their wounds, and later another of the prisoners that had been wounded, a man named George Metcalf, died. It was thought that injuries he received at Glenrowan had led to an infection that killed him.

Because the police had burned down the inn, Mrs. Jones and her children had lost everything they owned and were homeless. Mrs. Jones had also lost her way of making a living. For the next few weeks people would visit Glenrowan to look for souvenirs in the ruins of the inn, taking everything from bullets to bits of bone they thought might have been from one of the dead outlaws.

| 14 |

Ned Kelly on Trial

After Glenrowan, Ned was taken to the hospital in Melbourne Gaol to recover. While he was there, he was visited by his mother who was still serving her sentence in the women's section of the prison for attacking Constable Fitzpatrick. It was the first time they had seen each other since she had been sentenced in 1878, and they were only allowed to see each other for thirty minutes. When Ned's family and friends tried to get permission to see him, they were refused by the prison authorities. This made it difficult to prepare Ned's case for when he went to court.

Many of the injuries Ned had received during his capture were permanent and made it hard to do things like write and stand up for long periods. For months afterwards, the prison doctor was still removing bullets and shot from his body, and some would never be removed because it was too hard to get out.

When he was well enough, Ned was sent back to Beechworth for a committal hearing to see if there was a strong enough case for a full trial in the Supreme Court. It was only the night before that Ned was able to meet the lawyer who had been hired to defend him in court, whose name was David Gaunson.

On August 6, 1880, the hearing began. Constable McIntyre and others gave evidence about Ned's crimes while he was not allowed to say anything in his own defence. When Ned spotted an artist drawing a picture of him, he put a possum skin blanket over himself so the artist couldn't finish. People came from all over to try and catch a glimpse of Ned in court, and after several days of witnesses giving evidence, it was decided that he should go to the Supreme Court in Melbourne to be tried on the charge of murdering Constable Thomas Lonigan at Stringybark Creek.

Constable Thomas McIntyre.

Ned was sent back to Melbourne and was put on trial on October 28, 1880. The judge in the case was Sir Redmond Barry, who had also been the judge that sentenced Mrs. Kelly to three years hard labour. Ned was defended by a barrister named Henry Bindon, who was being assisted by David Gaunson. Once again, many witnesses came forward to share information about Ned's crimes, but the most important witness was Constable McIntyre. When it was suggested that the Jerilderie letter should be used as evidence, David Gaunson refused to allow it as Ned's admission in the letter to having shot and killed all three police at Stringybark Creek would have sealed his doom.

At the conclusion of the trial Ned Kelly was found guilty of murder. Before his sentence was handed down, Ned argued in the court with the judge and told him that one day they would go to a far greater court in the afterlife where they would see who was right and who was wrong. Right to the end Ned believed he was justified in his actions and was not afraid to die because of them. Sir Redmond Barry was angry that Ned did not seem to feel sorry for the people he had hurt through his actions and gave a long speech about the importance of making an example out of him so that other young people would not follow in his footsteps. He then sentenced Ned to be hanged until death, which was the usual punishment for such a crime, and Ned was returned to the gaol to await his execution. Before he was taken away, Ned told the judge, "I will see you there where I go!"

Sir Redmond Barry.

| 15 |

The End of Ned Kelly

As soon as Ned was sentenced to hang, his friends and family began to try and get the sentence changed. His sisters Maggie and Kate as well as his brother Jim, who had recently returned from New South Wales, were joined by Steve Hart's sister, Ettie, their cousins Tom and Kate Lloyd, and Wild Wright as they tried to save Ned's life. They got thousands of signatures on a petition, held marches in the city and met with politicians to try and get the sentence of death changed, but the decision was made to go ahead with the hanging.

The day before he was to be hanged, Ned was allowed to see his close family and posed for photographs so that his loved ones could have a last reminder of him. In one of the photographs, he is holding up the leg irons around his feet to show how defiant he was.

Ned poses for a portrait in the Melbourne Gaol.

On the morning of November 11, 1880, Ned Kelly was taken to the condemned cell and given the last rites before being restrained and walked onto the gallows of Melbourne Gaol and hanged for the murder of Constable Lonigan. It was said by some that his last words were, "Ah well, I suppose... Such is life."

After he died, his body was taken to a building in the gaol grounds called the "dead house". His hair and beard were shaved off so that a mould could be taken of his head for a death mask. The death mask was shown in the local wax museum next to a display of wax statues of the Kelly Gang in the "Chamber of Horrors".

Ned was buried in the courtyard of the gaol, where he would remain until most of the gaol was knocked down in the 1920s. When his coffin was discovered, people stole many of his bones, but they were made to return them. His remains were moved to Pentridge Prison where he was buried alongside the other inmates that had been hanged at Melbourne Gaol and Pentridge. After Pentridge closed, he was reburied for the last time in Greta Cemetery with his family.

Ellen Kelly lived until 1926, when she died at the age of 93. She had lived long enough to see Australia through the gold rush, Federation and the first World War. The last member of Ned's immediate family was his younger brother Jim, who died in 1946, just after the end of the second World War. Both Ellen and Jim would have been able to watch the silent films made about the Kellys, including *The Story of the Kelly Gang*, which was the first full-length feature film ever made in the world. They would have been able to listen to the radio and drive in cars, except that they were still terribly poor and could not afford such things. There are still relatives of the Kellys alive today and many of them live in the same places that the Kellys, Lloyds, Quinns and Harts lived in all those decades ago.

Ned Kelly has become one of Australia's most popular historical figures. Some people look at him as a hero that stood up for the poor people who were being bullied by the police and the wealthy squatters. Some other people see him as nothing more than a horrid villain who robbed banks, stole horses and murdered police.

Many items connected to him are on display in places like the Old Melbourne Gaol, the State Library of Victoria and the Victoria Police Museum. You can still visit many of the places where his story took place, including Glenrowan where he was finally captured. A memorial to the murdered police stands at Stringybark Creek near where they were camped in October 1878.

Ned Kelly has had more books, plays, films, songs, television shows, documentaries, and artworks made about him than just about any other person in Australian history. Because his story means so much to so many people it will probably never stop being shared and debated.

Ned Kelly the day before he was hanged 1880.
Source: State Library Victoria. 1648186, b26428

GLOSSARY

Legal Terms

Trial: If someone is accused of having committed a crime, they will be put on trial to either prove or disprove it. This often involves a judge or magistrate (who can decide on a punishment if the crime is proven), a jury (a group of people who will listen to the evidence and say whether they think that the person did commit the crime or not), the defendant (the person accused of a crime), witnesses who may have seen the crime committed, and lawyers who are in charge of proving the guilt of the defendant (prosecution) or disproving the accusations (defence).

Court: Trials are held in a court. There are different types of courts for different kinds of crime. In colonial era Victoria, the lowest level of crime would be tried in the Court of Petty Sessions or Police Court where a Police Magistrate (PM) or Justice of the Peace (JP), who may have had no legal qualifications, could make a decision on the case without a jury. These were crimes like property damage or unpaid debts. This was also where committal hearings were conducted to determine if there was enough evidence for the case to go to a higher court. The next level was the General Sessions (or Quarter Sessions as they were originally known) where the trial was conducted in front of a judge and jury. Crimes tried here were known as felonies and were of a more serious nature and could lead to the defendant going to gaol if they were found guilty. The Supreme Court is where the worst crime cases were put on trial, such as murder, and once again a judge and jury would oversee the trials. Capital crimes, those which were punishable by death, could only be tried in the Supreme Court.

Lawyer: A person who appears in court will usually be represented by a lawyer — a person educated in the legal system. There are two types of lawyers: solicitors, who usually work as part of a team or represent clients accused of lesser crimes; and barristers, who generally have higher qualifications and can represent clients in bigger cases, such as those that go to the Supreme Court.

Committal Hearing: This is where a magistrate will hear evidence of a crime to determine if it is worth taking the case to trial in a higher court.

Gaol: This is the old-fashioned way of spelling jail. The prisons built in Australia in the 1800s were named in this way. These were buildings designed to contain convicts or felons, the people who had been found guilty of committing crimes or felonies. Convicts were kept prisoner in tiny rooms called "cells".

Capital Punishment: The worst crimes were called capital crimes and the punishment for committing them was usually execution (death). In Australia, the only legal form of execution was hanging, where the condemned person (the felon sentenced to death) would be dropped through a trapdoor with a rope tightened around their neck to kill them. If someone was sentenced to death, they were allowed to lodge an appeal, which was a way of having the case re-examined and potentially having the death sentence reduced to something like life in prison. The appeal would go before a panel of judges called the Executive Council and their decision was final. After the condemned was dead their body would be buried within the gaol grounds.

Other Terms

Squatter: In the early days of the colonial period, some settlers would explore land and occupy it without permission from the government, which was called squatting. This allowed some farmers to become very wealthy because they could take control of all of the best farmland in an area without having to pay for it. The squatters were often livestock farmers, raising sheep or cattle. By the time of the gold rush the squatters had taken so much land there was a shortage for other farmers, which led to laws that restricted how much land someone could own and allowed people to purchase land from the squatters.

Selector: Poorer farmers were able to apply for a selection of Crown land (land that was owned by the British government) to establish a farm on. The selector did not own the land but could live and farm on it if they had the required licence. They were required to pay rent and cultivate the land and after seven years they could pay off the selection so that they owned it. Squatters often disliked selectors for being of a lower social class and using land that had once been in their possession. Selectors disliked squatters for stealing the best land for themselves and often felt like the squatters would pick on them to push them out of the area.

Sympathiser: People who showed sympathy for the outlaws were called Sympathisers. They were people who supported the gang either through their opinions or actions such as providing them information, food, horses, and shelter.

Pound (£): In colonial Australia the currency was based on the British system of pounds, shillings, and pence instead of the modern decimal system of dollars and cents. The pound symbol is based on a capital L which stood for the Latin term *libra pondo* (meaning a pound of money) because when the Romans occupied England, they brought their language with them as well as their currency. This is also why pence is represented by a letter d (for *denarius*) but is also why shillings are represented by s (for *solidus,* not shilling), which were also used in Australia.

BIBLIOGRAPHY

In all my years reading about Ned Kelly I have read so many books, news articles and historical documents that I've lost count. What I have listed here are just some of the books that I found most useful in my research over the years. I am sure that you will find them useful too. – Aidan Phelan

***

Jones, Ian, *Ned Kelly: A short life.* Second Edition. Hachette Australia, Sydney, New South Wales, 2003.

Molony, John N., *Ned Kelly.* Penguin Books, Melbourne, Victoria, 1989.

FitzSimons, Peter, *Ned Kelly: the story of Australia's most notorious legend.* Random House Australia, North Sydney, New South Wales, 2013.

Castles, Alex C. and Castles, Jennifer, *Ned Kelly's last days: setting the record straight on the death of an outlaw.* Allen and Unwin, Crow's Nest, New South Wales, 2005.

McMenomy, Keith *Ned Kelly: the authentic illustrated history.* Hardie Grant Books, South Yarra, Victoria, 2001.

BIBLIOGRAPHY

Toohill, Trudy, (editor of compilation.) *The reporting of Ned Kelly & the Kelly gang.* Boolarong Press, Salisbury, Qld, 2015.

Brown, Max, *Ned Kelly: Australian son.* Georgian House, Melbourne, Victoria, 1948.

Kelly, Ned & McDermott, Alex, (writer of introduction.) *The Jerilderie Letter.* The Text Publishing Company, Melbourne, Victoria, 2001.

Kieza, Grantlee, *Mrs Kelly: The astonishing life of Ned Kelly's mother.* Harper Collins Publishers, Sydney, New South Wales, 2017.

Passey, Kevin J., *In search of Ned: a travelogue of Kelly country.* Lachlan Publishing, Albury, New South Wales, 1988.

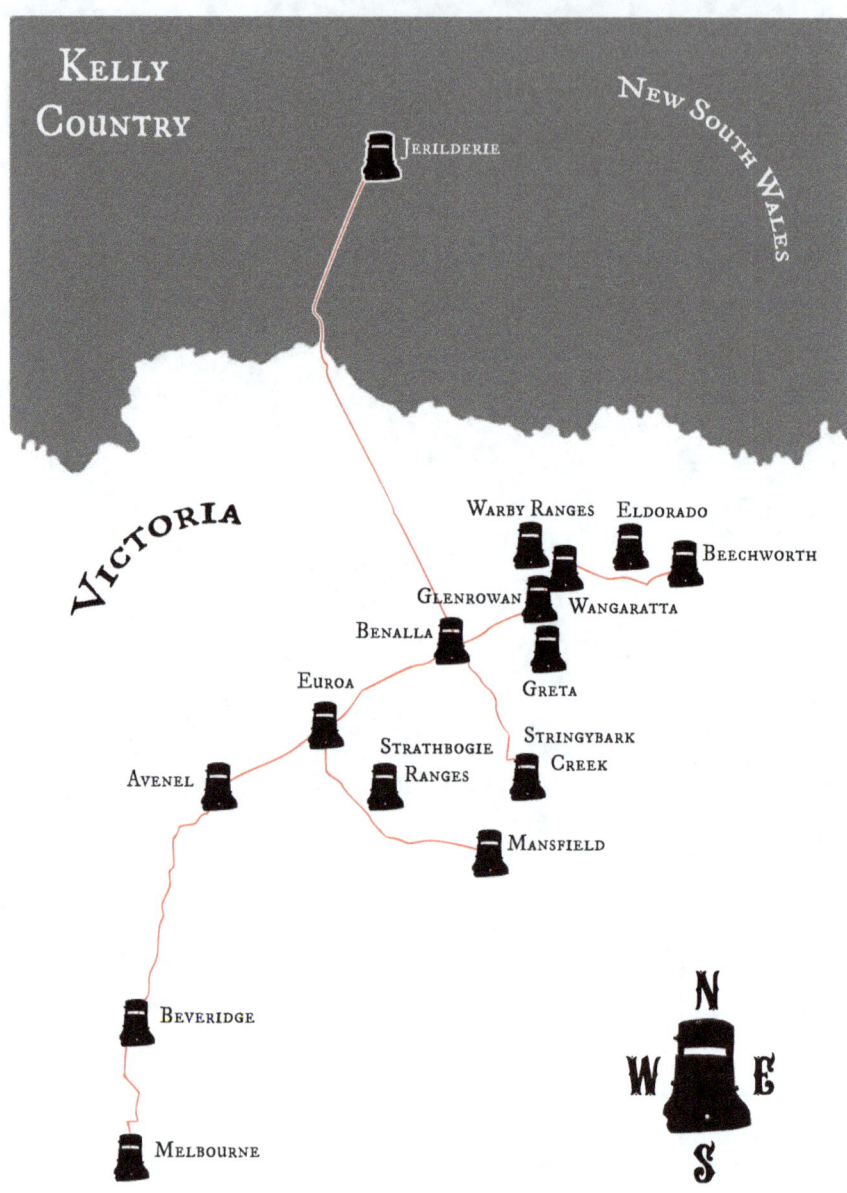

PLACES TO VISIT

Old Melbourne Gaol: This is where Ned Kelly was hanged, and his mother spent most of her prison sentence. There are many items on display related to Ned including his death mask, one of his revolvers and part of the scarf Thomas Curnow used to stop the police train.

State Library of Victoria, Melbourne: The state library was founded by Redmond Barry, the judge who sentenced Ned to death, because he believed everyone should have access to knowledge and education. The library has the largest collection of original images and documents related to the Kelly story, including the Jerilderie letter. They also have Ned Kelly's armour and one of his boots on display.

Victoria Police Museum, Melbourne: The Victoria Police have many fascinating objects on display, including a small number of the Kelly items in their collection. You can see Dan Kelly's and Steve Hart's armour as well as a bag Ned Kelly at Glenrowan.

The Kelly House, Beveridge: In Beveridge you can see a house that was built by Ned's father, Red Kelly, when the family lived in the village. It has recently been restored and landscaped.

Benalla Costume and Kelly Museum: The prized items in the collection of this museum include Ned's green silk sash, which he wore at Glenrowan and is said to have been given to him by the Shelton family after he rescued their son Richard from drowning, as well as an exact replica of Joe Byrne's armour. There are also the doors from the old Benalla lock-up as well as some smaller items believed to be connected to Ned Kelly.

Ned Kelly Discovery Hub, Glenrowan: This new, state-of-the-art facility introduces visitors to the Kelly story and the events of the Glenrowan siege. There are information panels, video presentations and a rooftop lookout.

Kellyland Glenrowan: This animated theatre and museum uses special effects, full scale dioramas and animatronics to take visitors back in time to the siege. The museum is full of unique items connected to local history as well as the Kelly Gang and Victoria Police such as firearms and police uniforms.

Kate's Cottage and Ned Kelly Museum, Glenrowan: The centrepiece of this attraction is a full scale, fully furnished replica of the Kelly house in Greta. There is also a museum which tells the Kelly story and shows many of the tools and equipment the Kelly family would have used around their home.

Beechworth Courthouse: This is where many of Ned's friends and family stood trial. The new upgrade scheduled to open in late 2023 will use audio visual displays to tell the stories of some of these trials.

Beechworth Gaol: This is where the Kellys and their associates spent time after committing crimes. Tours are frequently conducted through the site.

The Old Printery, Jerilderie: This is where Ned wanted his famous letter to be printed by the local newspaper editor. There are replica suits of the gang's armour on display and an exhibition about some of the local bushrangers. Afterwards, if you go on a stroll through town you will spot many of the buildings associated with the gang's visit there in 1879.

The Author

Aidan Phelan is the writer and historian for *A Guide to Australian Bushranging*, an online resource that has been bringing Australia's outlaw heritage to a worldwide audience since 2017. His first novel, *Glenrowan*, depicted the events leading to the capture and execution of Ned Kelly and has sold hundreds of copies around the world since its release in 2020. He has also published *Bushranging Tales: Volume One* (2022), *William Westwood in his own words* (2022) and *Aaron Sherritt: Persona non Grata* (2022).

Aidan has a Bachelor of Arts and a Diploma of Education, and studied writing and editing at what is now known as Melbourne Polytechnic. He was born and raised in the suburbs of Melbourne and developed a fascination with the story of Ned Kelly on his first visit to Glenrowan as a child in 1998. This soon grew to be a consuming passion for Australian history, culminating in the creation of *A Guide to Australian Bushranging* and the many books and related projects that he has worked on since then.

Aidan at Kate's Cottage in Glenrowan, aged 13.